The Three Wishes

Retold by Andrew Prentice

Illustrated by Lorena Alvarez

Reading consultant: Alison Kelly

Ben, a woodcutter, and his wife, Lara, lived in a magical forest.

Ben and Lara worked hard...

...but they were poor and often hungry.

"Yummy nettle soup again..."

Still, they had each other and that was enough.

One fine morning, Ben went off to work.

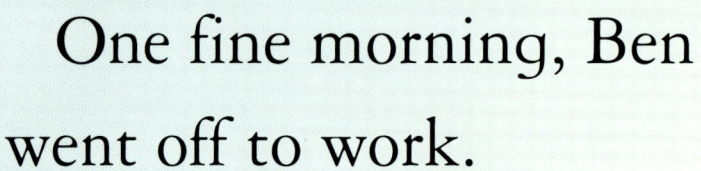

"Chop well, my love!"

He walked far into the woods.

He was looking for just the right kind of tree.

"This one is broad and tall!"

Ben got ready to cut it down.

Suddenly, a fairy popped out of the tree.

STOP!

"This is my home! Please don't cut it down," he cried.

"Oh!" said Ben. "I'm sorry."

The fairy was happy.

"You are a good, kind man," he said.

"Zap! Zing! Ting!"

"I have given you three wishes. You can wish for anything."

"*Anything?*" said Ben.

But the fairy had disappeared.

Ben hurried home.

"Lara will be so happy!" he thought.

"I want her to have everything.

Our lives will change forever."

"What shall we wish for first?

Maybe a new house..."

A marble palace?

A crystal castle…

A whole mountain made of gold!

Lara was not at home.
Ben was disappointed.

His tummy rumbled.
He imagined all the food
he could wish for.

Caverns of cheese...

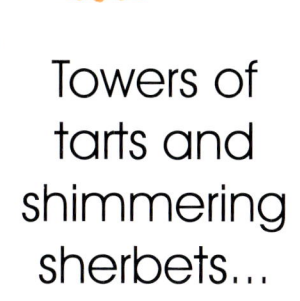

Towers of tarts and shimmering sherbets...

Sizzling six-foot sausages!

"I wish I had a sausage," Ben said to himself.

He heard the tinkle of
a silvery bell. A sausage
appeared on the table.

Oops!

It looked delicious.

Just then, Lara came home.

How did you get this amazing sausage?

"A fairy gave me three wishes!" Ben explained. "I wished for it, by mistake."

"You did what?" said Lara.

"I was hungry," said Ben.

"Doesn't it look delicious?"

"You are a silly man!"

Lara walked around the room, getting crosser and crosser.

"We still have two wishes left," said Ben.

"We'd have three if you weren't so silly!" said Lara.

"Would you like some sausage?"

"Argh! I wish that sausage was stuck to your nose!"

25

They both heard the sound of silvery bells.

"What's happened to your nose?" Lara screamed.

"What have you done?"
Ben was scared.

"I'm so sorry," said Lara.
"I didn't think."

Ben grabbed his nose.
It was soft and squishy!
He looked in the mirror.

A yummy smell filled his nostrils.

"Oh no!"

But he wasn't hungry any more.

"What are we going to do?" said Lara.

"I don't know," Ben whispered. "The sausage is stuck."

"We have to get it off!"
said Lara.

"Oh Ben, I'm so sorry."

They tried everything to get the sausage off his nose.

They tried tugging it.

They tried butter.

They even tried ice.

Nothing worked.

After several hours, the sausage was still stuck to Ben's nose.

"I can't live like this," Ben wailed.

"Everyone will laugh. I won't be able to leave the house ever again."

"You have to use the final wish," said Lara.

It's our only hope.

"But I wanted us to be rich," said Ben, "with plenty of cheese…"

"It's the last wish. Are you sure?"

"I'm sure. You need your old nose," said Lara. "I liked it."

"I wish for my nose to be normal," said Ben.

They both heard the sound of silvery bells.

Ben's nose was normal again.

The sausage was back
on the table.

"That's it then," said Ben.

"No more wishes," said Lara.

"Are you hungry?" said Ben.

They ate the sausage together.

It *was* delicious.

The cottage was warm and snug. The fire crackled.

Outside, it started to rain.

"I'm sorry about the palace," said Ben.

"I'm sorry about the cheese," said Lara.

"This will do just fine."

About the story

The Three Wishes is an old folk tale. Our version is adapted from Charles Perrault's story, which he first published in 1697.

Designed by Laura Nelson Norris
Series designer: Russell Punter
Series editor: Lesley Sims

First published in 2019 by Usborne Publishing Ltd., Usborne House, 83-85 Saffron Hill, London EC1N 8RT, England. www.usborne.com Copyright © 2019 Usborne Publishing Ltd. All rights reserved. No part of this publication may be reproduced, stored in a retrieval system or transmitted in any form or by any means, electronic, mechanical, photocopying, recording or otherwise, without the prior permission of the publisher. The name Usborne and the devices ⊕ ⊕ are Trade Marks of Usborne Publishing Ltd. UE. First published in America in 2019. EDC, Tulsa, Oklahoma 74146 www.usbornebooksandmore.com
Library of Congress Control Number: 2019945519